MONEY GUILT OR EXCITEMENT?

By Wilfred Bockelman

AUGSBURG PUBLISHING HOUSE
MINNEAPOLIS

MONEY: GUILT OR EXCITEMENT?
Stewardship in the Church

Developed under the auspices of Commitment to Mission, The American Lutheran Church

Cover art by Betty Sievert

International Standard Book No. 0-8066-2258-X

Manufactured in the United States of America

Contents

A word from the author

Authors have at least three thoughts in mind when they sit down to write a book.

First, they are convinced that they have something to say. In my case, that is pretty well expressed in the title of the book, *Money: Guilt or Excitement?* The cover further defines that this has to do with stewardship in the church. I am intrigued with the fact that in the business world, money often is associated with excitement; while in the church, it often is laden with guilt. Most congregations have an annual stewardship emphasis that lasts a week or a month. Yet, even the best of members are seldom totally happy about it. It's just something that has to be done. And the suggestion that money matters could be exciting is often met with the response, "Of course, the church is supposed to say that. That too is a part of stewardship month we have to endure." But that is precisely what I am suggesting in this book, that money can be exciting.

Secondly, an author has some kind of image of the people who will read the book. I realize that droves of people are not searching the bookstores for a book about stewardship and money. But I also realize that most churches have an annual stewardship emphasis and that they might be looking for some new ideas to stimulate their thinking.

I envision three groups of people reading the book: those responsible for the annual stewardship emphasis in the congregation, including the pastor, the official board of the congregation, and the stewardship committee. A smaller group of potential readers are those responsible on a national or regional scale for developing the program of the church and communicating it to members of congregations. A third group includes members of congregations, those who will be asked to contribute. I also can visualize the book being used in congregational adult forums as a basis for discussion about the use of money in the church.

Thirdly, authors generally have hopes of what will happen to people as a result of having read the book. Although the book is entitled *Money: Guilt or Excitement?*, it has more to do with excitement than with guilt. I hope that readers will be enriched with the exciting use of money.

—Wilfred Bockelman

1

MONEY—GUILT OR EXCITEMENT?

Why is it that talk about money can produce feelings as opposite as excitement and guilt? In the business world money is an exciting topic. In the days before daily newspapers had special sections on business and finance, those subjects often appeared in the section containing box scores and sports events.

The assumption (admittedly sexist) was that men would find equal excitement in sports and business. So papers made it easier for men to find these two subjects by putting them close together.

But in the church world, talk of money often is associated with guilt or, at least, an uncomfortable feeling. Most congregations have an annual stewardship emphasis lasting a week or a month. Members know it's coming. There are a few who really enjoy this opportunity to talk about the mission of the church and unabashedly ask for the money to support that mission. But for the most part, even the best of members are seldom totally happy about it: "It's something that just has to be done, so let's do it and get it over with."

A recent survey by a major denomination showed that 55 percent of those who had dropped out of church said as their major reason for leaving that there was too much talk in the church about money. It is possible, of course, that they were unhappy with their church anyway and too much talk about money was the easiest thing to blame. It is also possible that their lives had been so absorbed with possessions that even the slightest hint of guidance on how to use their money made them nervous, particularly if it was suggested that they support the church.

The church may do well to look at the way it talks about money. Even if the church is justified in calling attention to the danger of becoming a slave of money, it has associated money so much with negatives that lead to guilt that it has overlooked the positives that lead to excitement.

Reasons for guilt

There are times when clearly pointing out a negative can have a positive effect. We may harbor attitudes that make us feel guilty. We need to confront those attitudes. The Bible and personal experiences remind us that we frequently have failed to develop appropriate priorities before using our material goods.

Jesus had this to say:

> **"Do not lay up for yourselves treasures on earth, where moth and rust consume and where thieves break in and steal, but lay up for yourselves treasures in heaven, where neither moth nor rust consume and where thieves do not break in and steal. For where your treasure is, there will your heart be also. . . . No one can serve two masters; for either he will hate the one and love the other, or he will be devoted to the one and despise the other. You cannot serve God and mammon" (Matthew 6:19-21, 24).**

Jesus also told this story of the rich man:

> **"The land of a rich man brought forth plentifully; and he thought to himself, 'What shall I do, for I have nowhere to store my crops?' And he said, 'I will do this: I will pull down my barns, and build larger ones; and there I will store all my grain and my goods. And I will say to my soul, Soul, you have ample goods laid up for many years; take your ease, eat, drink, be merry.' But God said to him, 'Fool! This night**

your soul is required of you; and the things you have prepared, whose will they be?' So is he who lays up treasure for himself, and is not rich toward God" (Luke 12:16-21).

Like the disciples, most of us begin to feel guilty when we hear the story from Mark 12:

"And he sat down opposite the treasury, and watched the multitude putting money into the treasury. Many rich people put in large sums. And a poor widow came, and put in two copper coins, which make a penny. And he called his disciples to him, and said to them, 'Truly, I say to you, this poor widow has put in more than all those who are contributing to the treasury. For they all contributed out of their abundance; but she out of her poverty has put in everything she had, her whole living.'"

Added to these illustrations from the Bible are numerous stories we hear about people in extreme poverty in this country, as well as in churches in developing countries, who barely have a subsistence income and yet put us to shame in their generosity.

Guilt ought not simply to be swept under the rug and ignored. God does not overlook guilt. God deals with it, forgives it, and helps us to recognize our blessings. This interrelation of ourselves, our possessions, and our feeling of responsibility to God is a complex one. It is easy to grab on to a number of scripture passages, such as the ones just referred to, and use them as a hammer to drive people to give more. And while these passages should not be overlooked, they also need to be set in the wider context of the whole of the biblical message. When so doing, of course, we must recognize that there is always the danger of rationalizing, that we choose those passages that are more comforting to us rather than those that would accuse us. Nevertheless, truth is too big for one sentence. One of its glories is its many facets—some easily understood, some perplexing; some to our liking, others not.

There is, for instance, that difficult saying in Luke 18, where Jesus tells the rich young ruler, "Sell *all* that you have and distribute to the poor, and you will have treasure in heaven." If every individual were to take this literally, where finally would the production of goods to sell come from so that someone would indeed have something to give to the poor?

In Luke 19, one chapter later, Jesus encounters Zacchaeus, who makes a commitment to give *half* of his goods to the poor. Jesus accepts that with the assurance that "today salvation has come to this house."

Many, if not most, of us feel somewhat like the man who needed bigger barns to store all of his crops. (We would convert the crops into cash and invest it in stocks or bonds.) We can empathize with the rich young ruler. He had the nagging feeling that all was not well with his life, but he found the giving up of all his wealth too great a sacrifice. And yet, simply wallowing in that guilt is not likely to produce much of a change in attitude.

Is there another way to look at money that would be more conducive to getting people excited about using money for the church?

Money—an exciting invention

Money is a marvelously exciting invention. It makes possible the bringing back to life of something that, in a sense, was dead. Money enables you to spend yourself twice.

Let's keep the arithmetic simple. Suppose you work for someone and are paid $5 an hour. You use up an hour's worth of energy. In a very real sense, that is an hour of *you* that now is gone. But the invention of money makes it possible to bring that energy back to life. When your employer pays you, the energy that you expended is given back in the form of money. You can now spend that energy over again, and again, and again.

An executive of a large oil company once described money as "a convenient way of packaging my life and work in order to trade it over the counter for the life and work of others."

The invention of money makes it possible to become involved in activities all over the world. This adds to the sense of excitement. Once people make an investment, even a modest one, in the stock market, they tend to follow the daily market reports closely to see what happens to their investment. Has the stock gone up in value? If so, why? Is the company growing? If so, why? Should they place their investment elsewhere? Or, should they make additional investments?

There can, of course, be dangers in becoming so enamored with money that one loses all concern over whether the money is used for good purposes or evil ones. One can become so consumed in a passion for money that money becomes the master. But the possible wrong use of money should not dissuade us from the primary purpose of this book—to learn to enjoy the excitement of money and to celebrate the good things that money can do.

Once we are convinced of the fact that money can be good, that it can be enjoyed, that it can be exciting, then we can experience joy and excitement about the way we use money in the church.

Caught in a dilemma

This book has a twofold emphasis. The title includes the words *stewardship* and *money.* There are similarities and differences between the two. Money always has to do with stewardship. Stewardship has to do with more than money. And so, when the church conducts a stewardship program, it often is caught in a dilemma, because a part of the basic approach that relates stewardship to money is proper motivation for the use of money.

The traditional approach to stewardship motivation has been that we give in response to the love of God, who first loved us. This motivation applies not only to how we use our money, but also to how we use our time and our talents. Because people do not seem to be as sensitive to talking about the proper use of time and talents as they are about the proper use of money, talk about money is often soft-pedaled.

Some years ago a prominent church leader was assigned the task of writing an article on stewardship with specific emphasis on the stewardship of money. Even with this special assignment, he still fell into the trap of writing so much about the general subject of stewardship, and its biblical, all-inclusive base, that hardly more than a few paragraphs were devoted to money itself. The church feels so strongly about the importance of biblical stewardship that those responsible for stewardship programs call attention to the fact that they are not essentially fund-raisers.

A further dilemma is the possible loss of credibility with those who are not that much committed to the spiritual message of stewardship. They know, or at least they are quite sure they know, that the reason a member of the church is making a stewardship call on them is to ask for the annual financial pledge. So why not get right to the point instead of couching it in a lot of biblical and spiritual phraseology?

There is a saying that during the first 10 months of the year the church preaches biblical stewardship. But when the last two months come around and it seems that the budget may not be met, all the stops are pulled out. Key church leaders and pastors are urged to tell members of the congregation that they need to make a special effort to improve their contributions during these last months or the church will not make its budget and important mission programs will have to be cut.

There is another possible dilemma when church leaders say that if the cause is worthy, all that is needed is prayer. God will lay it on the hearts of people to support that need. A more careful look at the facts discloses that that is not the way it often happens. Even those who insist that all we need to do is pray still resort to frequent reminders and urgings, particularly as the end of the fiscal year draws near.

I am not saying that we shouldn't pray or that we shouldn't use good spiritual emphases. But motivations for giving are complex, and the Holy Spirit works through a combination of them. The apostle Paul himself appeals to a number of motivations. In 2 Corinthians 9 he encourages people along spiritual stewardship lines to give "not reluctantly or under compulsion, for God loves a cheerful giver." Just a few verses earlier, however, he resorts to shaming them. He tells the Corinthians that he boasted of their liberality to the Macedonians; now they had better come across "so that our boasting about you may not prove vain in this case, so that you may be ready, as I said you would be: lest if some Macedonians come with me and find you are not ready, we be humiliated—to say nothing of you." And just to be on the safe side, Paul sends a representative ahead to "arrange in advance for this gift you have promised, so that it may be ready not as an exaction but as a willing gift." After all that pressure, it may be a bit difficult to believe that the gift is still "willing."

Tithing—excitement or guilt

Tithing is another subject that can evoke either excitement or guilt. There are those who have committed themselves to tithing, giving the first tenth of everything they receive, and have found it pure excitement and fun. It removes a lot of stress from the weekly decision of "How large should I make the check to the church?" The decision has been made. The amount already is set aside. It's there. Only the fun remains of deciding where it can be used best and of watching it accomplish its purpose.

For others—particularly those whose income may be very low or very high—tithing is more of a problem that may lead to guilt. Someone on a very low income may have great difficulty believing that one-tenth of that already low amount can be spared for the church. They may have heard others say that "once you've tried tithing, you'll never go back to giving less than a tithe." But somehow that doesn't seem to work for them and, in fact, may increase their own guilt feelings. They also believe the promises of God that God will indeed provide for all their needs. But what does one do when doctor bills pile up and the children need shoes?

Others in the high-income bracket may have equal problems of trying to sweep guilt under the rug of common sense and rationalization. When they were making $25,000 a year, it seemed possible to give $2500 to the church. But now that they are making $100,000 a year, must they really give $10,000 away?

Further questions have to do with various interpretations of tithing. Some Old Testament readings indicate that a tithe was just a beginning point and that for the really faithful people of God, a double and triple tithe were expected. And what is to be included in the tithe? In the Old Testament, part of the tithe was used to take care of older people of the community. Could our taxes, part of which is used to take care of people in need, or our Social Security contributions be included as part of our tithe? (The tithe will be discussed further in Chapter 7.)

All of these questions have an edge about them, an edge that tends toward guilt and, therefore, elicits a tendency not to want to discuss giving. But we are aware that we do have to talk about it. What would it be like, however, if we could talk about money with the same sense of excitement as in the business world?

2

A THEOLOGICAL BASIS FOR STEWARDSHIP

It is understandable that talk about money in the church should be done in a context of stewardship based on the Bible. Crass commercialism conceivably could bring large sums of money into the church's treasury, but that would be out of keeping with what the church stands for. Some would even go so far as to say that having "money-raising events," such as suppers, bazaars, car washes, and ticket sales—all of which often depend on outsiders to help pay the cost of running the church—is not in keeping with good stewardship. Opinions vary: I'll say more about that later.

In some church circles the use of "professional fundraisers" is questioned. Even though they may be successful in raising more money than the church would have without them and even though there may be nothing dishonest about the way the money is raised, the accusation often is made that they resort to "high-pressure tactics" not in keeping with good "biblical stewardship."

But the two need not necessarily be mutually exclusive. Is it possible to do both, combine the best of biblical teaching with some of the successful methods used by the so-called professional fundraisers that are not antibiblical.

What do we mean by theological?

Some people are afraid of the word *theology.* "Just give me the simple Bible," they say. "Don't confuse me with theology, which is a lot of talk in big words that

I can't understand. And anyway, theology deals with people's opinions and pits one person's opinion against that of another."

But there is no such thing as not having any theology. There may be good theology or bad theology, but there is no *no* theology. Theology comes from two Greek words: *theos,* which means "god"; and *logos,* which means "word." Theology, then, is words about God. We read the Bible and see what it says about God, and then we say in our own words what we understand the Bible to say. That's our theology.

Sometimes things are said very clearly in a verse or two. At other times verses seem to stand in tension with verses in other parts of the Bible. That does not mean one is right and the other wrong. It simply means that in our theology we need to struggle to understand meanings. And if it should be that two people come to different conclusions, that does not always mean that one is totally right and the other totally wrong. (We, of course, have a tendency to think that the one who comes closest to what we have been taught to believe is right.) It's good that we are saved by the grace of God and not by the certainty that we have the right answers at all times.

So what does the Bible have to say about money or possessions? We have already referred to this several items in the first chapter. Money can develop an inordinate power over a person; it can hold a person in virtual slavery. "You cannot serve God and mammon," Jesus said. We sometimes translate *mammon* as "money" or "wealth," but it is more than that. It is an obsession with money as that which gives us security. It is money as an object of worship and greedy pursuit, a personification of evil.

Nowhere does the Bible say that having money—even lots of it—is in and of itself wrong. One of the commandments, "Thou shalt not steal," was given to assure people the right of ownership to possessions.

Some of Jesus' friends were wealthy. It is assumed that Nicodemus, who came to Jesus by night, was wealthy (John 3). Joseph of Arimathea, who provided the tomb in which Jesus was laid, evidently was wealthy. Abraham had great wealth. Jesus allowed Zacchaeus to keep half of his wealth, after he had paid back fourfold all those he had cheated.

True, Old Testament prophets did indeed rail against the wealth of their day: "Woe to those who join house to house, who add field to field, until there is no more room" (Isaiah 5:8). Or listen to the sixth chapter of Amos:

> **"Woe to those who lie upon beds of ivory, and stretch themselves upon their couches, and eat lambs from the flock, and calves from the midst of the stall; who sing idle songs to the sound of the harp, . . . who drink wine in bowls, and anoint themselves with the finest oils."**

But in each of these cases it is not the wealth as such to which the Bible objects, but the use to which people put it and their callousness to the poor.

Even the most pious of Christians have a tendency to be quite selective about the scripture passages they memorize. How many have not been greatly comforted and thankful that they memorized Isaiah 1:18:

> **"Come now, let us reason together, says the Lord: though your sins are like scarlet, they shall be as white as snow; though they are red like crimson, they shall become like wool."**

Why was there no emphasis put on memorizing Isaiah 1:16-17?

> **"Wash yourselves; make yourselves clean; remove the evil of your doings from before my eyes; cease to do evil, learn to do good; seek justice, correct oppression; defend the fatherless, plead for the widow."**

Throughout, the Bible teaches that those who have great wealth also have responsibility to use it properly. Over and over again it calls for special consideration for the poor, the widows, the orphans, the defenseless, and the refugees in the land. The Bible is not always specific about how this is to be done; and where it does give specific instructions, they relate to the culture and regulations of that day.

For instance, farmers were not allowed to reap the corners of their fields; if they did they would be stealing. Orchard owners were not allowed to go through a second time to pick what wasn't ripe the first time. That was for the poor to come and get. That was part of the structure of that society for taking care of the poor.

Our society is obligated to find ways equally effective for taking care of the poor among us. That's what ethics is all about. Christianity teaches that God cares very much that the poor be taken care of and that it is an obligation of the wealthy to find ways of doing so. The ways in which that is done may vary. It may not mean an outright dole. But God places on us the obligation to establish structures of society to take care of the needy. It is a part of our theology. And since such structures involve money, usually large sums of it, money becomes a theological question.

Another aspect of Christian theology is mission. It is part of God's plan that God's message be proclaimed to all the world. In the Christian church this is understood as mission, most clearly announced in Matthew 28:18-20:

> **"And Jesus came and said to them, 'All authority in heaven and on earth has been given to me. Go therefore and make disciples of all nations, baptizing them in the name of the Father and of the Son and of the Holy Spirit, teaching them to observe all that I have commanded you; and lo, I am with you always, to the close of the age.' "**

Another version of Jesus' commission is found in Acts 1:8:

> **"But you shall receive power when the Holy Spirit has come upon you; and you shall be my witnesses in Jerusalem and in all Judea and Samaria and to the end of the earth."**

It is this gigantic mission enterprise that the church has in mind when it asks its people for money. Now the question becomes, how can Christians best be motivated to provide this money? Is just having the money enough? If so, we could resort to simple fund-raising. Or, how much do we also insist on proper biblical, theological motivation for giving money? That is what stewardship education is about.

At this point the church has sometimes—perhaps unwittingly—appealed to guilt as a motivation: "You ought to put at least as much in the offering plate on Sunday morning as you spent on dinner and a concert or movie on Saturday night." Maybe so, maybe not.

When the church has appealed to the excitement of giving (which indeed it has done) it often has blunted that approach by using only one emphasis. To change the metaphor, it often has played and replayed one string, when there are at least three that could provide exciting music.

Stewardship motivation based on redemption

Liturgical churches have the creedal statement of the Apostles' Creed, which provides a workable outline for discussion. The creed is divided into three articles—the first of which deals with God the Creator, the second with Christ the Redeemer, and the third with the Holy Spirit and the church.

Many approaches to stewardship education have emphasized the second article. God loves us and sent Jesus

Christ to die for us, thus making possible the forgiveness of sins and redemption. Out of a thankful heart to God who has redeemed us we should now share our wealth with the church so that others may hear this good news also. It is perhaps expressed best in Martin Luther's explanation to that article:

> **I believe that Jesus Christ, true God, begotten of the Father from all eternity, and also true man, born of the virgin Mary, is my Lord. He has redeemed me, a lost and condemned creature, purchased and won me from all sin, from death and from the power of the devil; not with silver and gold but with his holy, precious blood, and with his innocent suffering and death; that I may be his own, live under him in his kingdom, serve him in everlasting righteousness, innocence and blessedness; even as he is risen from the dead, lives and reigns to all eternity. This is most certainly true.**

God, through Christ, has done all of these things for us. Now, in return, we should thank him. That becomes the motivating force behind our stewardship. Traditionally, three ways have been suggested in which we can carry out our stewardship—through the proper use of time, talents, and possessions. We give of our time to serve in the church and in other worthwhile organizations. We consider our talents as to where we can use them best.

This is sometimes referred to as "pure" stewardship, based totally on a response to God's love. In a sense it would make no difference what the need might be, because you don't give to support a need. You give purely in response to God's love. According to this approach, if it were taken to its logical conclusion, there would be no need to depict in graphic terms what the needs are or what successes have been achieved by money given in the past or what could be done if the church only had more money.

Stewardship education based on creation

Giving motivated in response to our redemption through God's love and grace is indeed a basic cornerstone to all stewardship education. It can be enhanced, however, if it is extended to include the other two articles of the Apostles' Creed. In their attempt to be totally Christ-centered, churches may neglect other equally biblical emphases.

Theologian Joseph Sittler warns that we "ought not to be more Christ-centered than Christ himself was. After all, he himself said that his purpose for coming into the world was to show us the Father." What, then, are some other teachings about the Father that the incarnation implies for us?

The first article of the Apostles' Creed presents God as Creator. In recent years, particularly with the emphasis on ecology, increasing attention has been paid to the assignment God gave at the time of creation. Is it possible to hold two assignments from God on an equal level without insisting that one takes precedence over the other? Or, is it possible that at certain times in history or for certain people one assignment may be more attractive and important than the other? May it even be that God equips some people with special gifts in one area and others with special gifts in another? And would our stewardship education and motivation be improved if we tried to match certain tasks with specific interests and abilities?

Jesus did indeed give his disciples the great missionary command to preach the gospel to all nations. This single command of Christ ought to motivate us to dedicate time, talents, and possessions so that the gospel may be spread throughout the world.

But the Creator, whom Jesus came to mirror for us, also gave a command to Adam and Eve to "tend the garden," to care for the earth. And that command has not been retracted. It is indeed a very exciting command. For some people the command growing out of creation has more motivating force than the command growing out of redemption. That does not mean that people should put all their energy into one and none in the other. Some churches, unfortunately, have a tendency to say that stewardship motivated by creation is not as worthy as stewardship motivated by redemption.

Quite frankly, this book is intended to excite people with large gift potential. These may indeed be the very people who are excited by a Creator God. And, in a sense, creation did not end with the sixth day. The assignment to care for the garden is a continuing one. Adam and Eve, and through them all human beings, were created to use their ingenuity and imagination. Some say using our imaginattion is what it means to be made in the image of God.

The assignment to care for the earth includes the call to use the imagination to design structures of society that care for the increasing billions of people on the earth. This is a complex task indeed. But it may be that its very complexity is thrilling and exciting to highly talented business and professional people who think in bigger terms than merely meeting a local congregational budget of $50,000 or $100,000 or even $1,000,000.

It is reasonable for a congregation of 2000 members, with literally scores of highly paid corporate executives and other people of means, to have a million dollar budget. The fact that the budget is not more or that even that amount is arrived at only after much pleading may indicate that the church has not yet captured the sense of excitement that includes creation, as well as redemption, as a motivation for stewardship.

Stewardship education based on fellowship

The third article of the Apostles' Creed is, perhaps, a little harder to grasp than the first and second articles as a motivation for stewardship. But it is powerful indeed when properly understood:

> **"I believe in the Holy Spirit, the holy catholic (universal) church, the communion of saints, the forgiveness of sins, the resurrection of the body, and the life everlasting."**

At least four elements stand out as awe-inspiring motivations for stewardship. We may have a little difficulty imaging the Holy Spirit, but the Spirit certainly is an intimate, abiding presence of God, not limited to activity within the walls of a church building.

The holy catholic church and the communion of saints refer to the unbelievably large body of believers throughout the world, who are like-minded and yet so different in many ways, that inspire us.

The reference to the forgiveness of sins may have a guilt-inducing association. But it also reminds us of our human condition. Finding ourselves bonded with others the world over, rich and poor, can become a powerful stimulus for action that requires large sums of money.

The resurrection of the body and the life everlasting is often a scary concept. Others, however, respond to these kinds of thoughts, particularly if they are approached with a sense of awe rather than with the idea of damnation and hell-fire.

The images conjured up in the third article of the Apostles' Creed can produce a powerful motivation for financial stewardship. There is a twofold emphasis on relationships. Generally we have conceived of the missionary task of the Western church as giving or sending, and the people and churches of the Third World as receiving.

Years ago that concept held a greater degree of truth. When missionaries came back from Asia and Africa and the Pacific Islands they had powerful stories to tell.

The stories often were told in three parts, accompanied by slides or movies of various quality. The first part of the story generally depicted some dreadful situation in those countries. Some of the people lived in a stone-age culture in the middle of the 20th century. Some were still cannibals. They had rather fierce appearances, carried spears, wore bones in their noses and ears, and covered themselves with multi-colored grease paint. They were deathly afraid of magic and suffered from disease.

Then the missionaries brought the gospel. The work was slow at first. But after years of persistent effort and many hardships on the part of missionaries, conversions came. The church was established.

The third series of pictures showed the results of this missionary work. Spears were laid down. Decorative bones were taken out of noses and ears. People began wearing different clothes. They gave up cannibal habits. Diseases were healed.

These were success stories. The gospel has that kind of power. And that kind of success had a motivating force to people to support "foreign missions." (Today it's more likely to be called world mission or global mission.) The success stories that come these days are often not as dramatic as those of people who dropped their spears and ceased being cannibals.

Yet, in another sense, the stories of world mission today are even more exciting. There are evidences that the gospel did indeed bring a new life. The work of the missionaries was successful, because churches were established in the developing nations. Now they are developing a strength of their own. They still need our help. But it is a different kind of help and it brings a different kind of reward.

No longer are we only senders; we also are receivers. These new Christians have things to teach us. They are now a real part of our family, of our community, of the community of saints. So we have exchange programs. Some of them come to our country. An increasing number of our people visit their countries. We also work together on projects.

In this country, we are learning the power of intercultural and interracial relationships. That is what the third article of the Apostles' Creed means by "the communion of saints." We actually see how we can work together. This means, of course, that the communication and world mission departments of the national church have the task of interpreting this work and mission to our people. And when they do, it can be exciting.

No longer is our *only* motive for financially supporting the church an expression of thanks for our own salvation and redemption. That is still one motive. But another motive is the joy and excitement we experience as we see the growing fellowship of countries and races and cultures enriching each other.

Any one of the three articles of the Christian faith, as expressed in the Apostles' Creed, is incomplete unless it is related to the others. The church often has impoverished itself by basing virtually all of its motivation for stewardship as stemming from the second article, which speaks of redemption.

Even those people who are motivated by their redemption and contribute to the church so that others may share that redemption experience a real excitement from seeing young churches formed among the newly converted, churches in which the Holy Spirit is at work.

In our endeavor to give due praise to God and for fear of succumbing to pride, we find it hard to say that we actually help God accomplish the divine task of keeping society going. But it is true! Surely that is exciting! This understanding can do more to make Christians increase their contributions to the church and similar causes than an *exclusive* reliance on the motivation of thanksgiving.

3

STEWARDSHIP AND GIVING—RELATED BUT DIFFERENT

The Bible uses the word *give* or one of its forms—*giving*, *gave*, *gifts*—more often than it does the word *stewardship*. The purpose of this chapter is not to argue that one is more important than the other. Both words are important, and while there is a relationship between them, this relationship is often blurred.

Basic to an understanding of stewardship is the concept that what we spend is actually not ours for ownership. It has been lent to us to invest, and a return is expected. People in the business and corporate world may understand this concept better than the stewardship that preachers and church officials try to teach.

Corporate executives realize that the capital with which they work is not their own. It has been lent them by stockholders who expect a return on their investment. Corporations are in the everyday business of being held responsible for the use of someone else's money. Stewardship teaching programs in the church often don't take advantage of this situation that exists in the lives of many of their members. Church leaders can be so insistent on using biblical language that they are unaware of the immediate illustrations they could use from the present day.

It goes against the grain of much stewardship teaching to ease up on the emphasis on giving. But if we take stewardship seriously, it is by definition *not* giving, because what we have is not our own. It is someone else's; it belongs to God. And if it already belongs to God, we can't *give* it back to God; but we can *invest* it for God.

It can bring returns. And even though the returns belong to God, we can enjoy the fact that we helped make them possible.

Remember the story of the talents. The master specifically asked the servants to "trade" what he had left them, to invest it so that it could bring a return.

I do not assume that simply changing the word *giving* to *investing* will suddenly move people substantially to increase their financial support of the church. An argument used against emphasizing the investing concept is that it appeals to selfishness. I invest because *I* want to get a return. That is true when I invest what I consider to be my own money for the sake of bringing me the best possible return. That is not true in the best understanding of stewardship.

The cynic may find it hard to believe that many corporate executives understand that they are indeed managers of someone else's funds. These executives understand that it is their obligation to manage those funds in such a way that the stockholders will make a good return. They also know that they have an obligation to their employees, to their customers, and to the communities in which they are located. Naturally, they are pleased that, if they are successful, they also will benefit personally. Many business managers do have a high sense of obligation to others, and they experience an excitement in the returns their management is bringing to others, as well as to themselves.

That does not mean that we shouldn't emphasize giving at all. As a matter of fact, giving is extremely important, and it can be just as exciting as investing. But it is important that the distinction be made between giving and investing. Each of them relates to joy and excitement and stewardship in a different way.

A broader understanding of stewardship emphasizes that stewardship includes not just the money you give to or invest in the church, but to all the money you spend and how you spend it. If you don't spend enough money for food or clothing, you aren't exercising good stewardship. If you don't spend any money on recreation, you very likely are not exercising good stewardship. And if you don't buy your spouse or a close friend a rose or some other kind of gift from time to time, you probably are exercising poor stewardship.

Not only are you responsible for the money you spend; you are also responsible for your body, for your family, and for all those things that make family life wholesome. So you should not feel guilty if you go to the movies or a concert, or take a vacation. These activities are important for a healthy, well-rounded life.

A church program of stewardship education should give just as much emphasis to the appropriate amount to be devoted to family and personal health as to the amount that should be given to the church.

To be sure, if you spend so much money on movies or trips that you don't have enough to buy food for a balanced diet, you are not exercising good stewardship, not because you are spending money for movies that you should be giving to the church, but because you are spending money for movies that you should be spending for food or for your children's education.

The gift of liberality

Liberality or the enjoyment of giving is itself a gift. People have it in varying degrees; but it can also be cultivated. There are those people for whom it is naturally easy to give—not only to church, but also to other people at various opportunities. They wouldn't think of not giving gifts at Christmas or on birthdays—not because they want something in return, but because it is just their nature to give and to enjoy giving.

They don't need the admonition of Luke 6:38:

> **"Give, and it will be given to you: good measure, pressed down, shaken together, running over, will be put into your lap. For the measure you give will be the measure you get back."**

That verse is not necessarily a cause-and-effect inducement to give. It simply describes what happens to the person who gives.

At times liberal giving may be an example of bad stewardship. People can give out of selfish motives, simply because they enjoy it so much, and not take into account the effect too many gifts may have on the receiver. Or, people may enjoy giving to others because in so doing they develop power over them. But, on the whole, it is far healthier to enjoy giving than to be niggardly.

People who find it easy to give and who enjoy giving will find it easier to give to the church. But even that joy can be enhanced when the gift takes on the character of an investment. For that to occur, the church must do a good job of interpreting to the giver that the gift is indeed an investment. Someone else may receive the dividends, but the joy of knowing that something important is being done with the money given and that it's producing dividends for someone gives a sense of satisfaction.

Again, it is not a matter of one approach being better than the other or bringing more joy than the other. It is simply a recognition that different people are motivated by different approaches. The church needs to feel comfortable with the fact—and to rejoice in it—that more than one approach can be used to motivate people to give financial support. To use the investment metaphor is a totally acceptable, biblical approach to teaching stewardship of money for the support of the church.

A good reason for the giving approach is that it can cultivate unselfishness. A human being is a social creature whose purpose is best fulfilled when he or she recognizes a relationship of interdependence with others. Living only to oneself has a stifling effect on the personality, simply because that is contrary to human nature. A person needs to give. A deliberate refusal to relate to others in a give-and-take relationship is a denial of who and what we are. What applies to the individual also applies to groups of individuals. One such group, a congregation, can also become ingrown, selfish, and thus unhealthy.

Approaching the stewardship of money in financial support of the church from the viewpoint of investing provides a powerful educational device that can bring added joy and excitement to those who support the church liberally. This, of course, imposes an obligation on those responsible for teaching stewardship on the congregational, regional, national, and global level. They will need to describe the work of the church at all levels in a way that is exciting.

The strengths and weaknesses of a 50-50 goal

Many congregations are developing what they call a 50-50 goal, giving (or investing) half of their budget in a local program and the other half in a national or worldwide program, often called "benevolence," which means "desiring to do good for others."

The 50-50 goal has some strengths and weaknesses. Its major strength is that congregations recognize themselves as part of a larger enterprise. They develop vision and deliberately structure their programs to express that vision. It may be, however, that local needs seem more pressing. A responsible approach might hold that for the present there is greater need for financial support of a local program than of a global program. If, after careful consideration, some congregation arrives at that conclusion, it should not automatically be put down as not living up to a 50-50 goal. The congregation needs to be reminded, however, that it easily can fall victim to a narrow, selfish view that always puts self first and thus miss the excitement of participating in a worldwide program.

Another possible danger of the 50-50 goal is a possible undermining of the importance of mission in the local community. Money given to the congregational budget is used to pay the pastor's salary, to buy educational materials for the congregation, and to meet such prosaic expenses as light and heat.

At least part of the money sent to the national and worldwide program of the church will go to pay the salary of a church executive who works in a national or international office, perhaps preparing educational material for people in other parts of the world. The building in which he or she works also needs heat and light. Is the money to pay for these necessities in a national office any more holy than the money used for the same purposes in the local congregation? Or is the money used for an overseas missionary's salary any more holy than the salary paid to the pastor of a congregation in the United States?

The process a congregation goes through to determine what percentage of its budget should go to local and national ministries may be more important than the final decision itself. There may be times when the budget ought to be 30-70 or 70-30. To arrive at an appropriate figure a congregation may be helped more by using the investment model than the giving model.

The church needs both givers and investors, and all people ought to do some of both—looking upon some of their contributions as pure gifts, without strings attached, and trusting that the church will use them responsibly; and looking on others as an investment in the kingdom of God and being excited about the "dividends" the investment will pay for others. The two are not mutually exclusive.

4

THE CHURCH AND THE WORLD—DIFFERENT BUT RELATED

One of the problems of the English language is that the same word is often used for concepts or objects that are quite different. This poverty of our language, for instance, is one of the factors that has caused such distress for those who feel that changing translations of the Bible to avoid sexist terms is doing violence to the Scriptures.

English has one word with two separate meanings for which Greek has two words. *Anthropos* is the Greek word for "humankind" or "humanity"; *aner* is the Greek word for "man," referring to male gender. English often translates both of them as "man."

The Germans likewise have two words. *Mensch* means "humankind"; *Mann* means "male-gender man." English again translates them both as "man."

There is a similar situation with the word *world*, particularly with the way the word is used in the Bible. Sometimes *world* refers to the universe; other times it means the planet earth; still other times it may mean all the people who live on this planet; and still other times it may refer to evil people or the forces of evil.

In the baptismal rites of some churches, sponsors speaking in behalf of the infant to be baptized or adults speaking for themselves are asked to renounce "the devil, the *world*, and the flesh."

We are told in John 3:16 that God loved the world; whereas in 1 John 2:15 we are told:

> **"Do not love the world or the things in the world. If any one loves the world, love for the Father is not in him."**

Jesus, in the prayer for his disciples, prays:

"The world has hated them because they are not of the world, even as I am not of the world. I do not pray that thou shouldst take them out of the world, but that thou shouldst keep them from the evil one" (John 17:14-15).

Obviously, we have to be careful with the way we use the word *world*, and what kind of activities we describe as worldly. There was a time when it seemed quite easy to point out worldly activities. Dancing, drunkenness, going to the movies, using cosmetics, and playing cards were all described by various groups of people as worldly. Their definition of worldliness was activities that opposed God, and they could be quite selective about the activities they put in that category. While they might grant that being unkind to people or gossiping also opposed God, they seldom expressed the same vehemence when denouncing those sins. And it may never have occurred to them that the height of worldliness might be an attitude so morose about the condition of the world that others conclude from observing them that God had lost charge or that there might not even be a God anymore, at least not a God strong enough to win the final victory.

So, when we talk about the church and the world in the area of stewardship, we need to be clear what meaning of *world* we are using. The church and the world are two categories. Both are important. Both have to do with stewardship. But sometimes they are kept totally separate. There are also times and reasons for bringing them closer together.

We go back to Genesis and the story of God's creation of the world, fully aware that the word used there is *earth* and not *world*. But we often use such expressions as "God made the world" and then, using the same word, warn that the church is quite distinct from the world and that things that work in the world ought not to be too readily approved for use in the church.

In Chapter 2 we already referred to the strong motivation for stewardship found in the creation story. God created the earth, filled it with plants and animals, and then put Adam and Eve and all humankind after them on the earth and told them to take care of it. For purposes of further discussion, let's call that place "world," the place in which all people—and for the purposes of this book, particularly Christians—are to carry out their God-given task.

Another word with a slightly different meaning, but which is very important in understanding the assignment given to Christians, is the word *nations.* That's the word used in the great missionary command Jesus gave to his disciples when he said, "Go therefore and make disciples of all nations" (Matthew 28:19).

And this introduces another important word, *mission.* We hear it so much these days, almost too much so that it loses some of its power. When we are sent on a mission, we are sent by someone who has authority to tell us what to do. We may or may not personally agree with the task, but that is beside the point when we are on a mission. Our assignment is to do what the one with the authority to send us wants us to do.

The problem—and also the challenge—in understanding our mission is that it is really a twofold mission. God's original assignment to Adam and Eve (and hence to all of us), to care for the world has not been retracted. It stands side by side with the mission given by Christ that we bring the gospel to the whole world. At times these two missions are close together; at times they seem to be somewhat at odds with each other. The challenge for the Christian is to be faithful to both missions.

These two missions have been described in various ways. Sometimes one is called *material,* the other *spiritual.* At times the words *sacred* and *secular* are used, or *church* and *world,* or *church* and *society,* or *present life* and *eternal life.*

Various analogies and illustrations are used to distinguish between them. Basic to all of these illustrations is the tension that exists between the two. This tension is not automatically bad; tension is the essence of life. We stay alive only because we have a large, pear-shaped muscle in the left-center of our rib cage that *tenses* and relaxes about 70 times a minute. The only way we can raise an arm in a steady motion is for one muscle to tense against another muscle.

In the Christian church these days, a tension is often perceived between evangelism and social action. This is a healthy tension because both are necessary; but this tension brings with it a problem for supporting the church financially. Those who feel strongly that more attention should be given to evangelism than to social action may cut their support if they feel too much attention is being given to social action. Those devoted to social action may think that it too is an expression of evangelism and sometimes channel their support away from the church and toward organizations active in the social action arena.

The following analogy illustrates these two points of view. Picture life on earth as a long ride on a passenger train whose destination is heaven. The train makes many stops along the way. The activities of a strongly evangelistic church is to get as many people as possible on the train at each of the stops, so that when the train arrives in heaven, it will be filled.

Those with a strong bent for social action are concerned about the condition under which people must live while they are on the train. Why are some riding in posh first-class accommodations with dining room facilities, air-conditioned cars and comfortable seats, while others are crowded into stuffy cars with hard-backed seats and no dining facilities?

The evangelists may argue: "Of course, we regret that there are such inequities, but they will last only for a while. In this life there always will be a certain amount of unpleasantness, even pain and suffering. But it is eternity that counts. The main thing is that the people are on the train when it arrives in heaven."

One problem with that argument is that it often excuses injustices in society with the argument that everything will be all right in heaven. That kind of logic allowed many Christians to approve of slavery and racial injustice in the nation.

A continuing tension between those two points of view is wholesome. It forces both sides constantly to rethink their positions in the light of the truth of the other viewpoint.

God's assignment to Adam and Eve and their descendants to "tend the garden" included far more than simply tilling the ground, planting seeds, pulling weeds, harvesting, and making sure that all the animals were fed. It included taking care of all the structures that make up a society and enable people to live together harmoniously.

The church indeed plays an important role in that assignment. But so do some other institutions in society. Each needs to recognize what the other can do.

A man who conducts seminars on the meaning of Christian vocation tells that one night during one of his presentations, a slightly past middle age man started to cry. He asked him if there was anything he would like to say, and the man told this story:

> **When I was a teenager and went to my first Bible camp, the pastor in charge of the camp told us the first day, "This week I would like all of you to give serious consideration to dedicating yourself to full-time service to the Lord. You pray about it. And if you come to the conclusion that you want to do so, you whisper that into my ear next Friday night at the campfire. I will announce that to the group and we will all pray for you."**

I wondered all week how I would handle that challenge. Friday night came. At the campfire, one boy went up and said he wanted to be a missionary. The pastor announced that and we all prayed for him. Another said he wanted to be a youth worker in the church. One girl wanted to be a parish worker. We prayed for all of them. Finally I went up and whispered into his ear that I wanted to be a teacher.

"A teacher of what? Religion?" the pastor asked.

"No I want to be a science teacher," I said.

"Well, that doesn't count," the pastor said.

"I taught science for 40 years in the high schools of Brooklyn," the man said as he wiped another tear from his eye, "and this evening is the first time that my work has ever been recognized as full-time service to the Lord."

I'm sure that deep down in his heart, even the pastor knew and believed that this faithful high school teacher was serving the Lord by teaching science. But his response indicates what often happens when the church calls for commitment to its cause. It fails to give proper recognition to organizations outside the church that also are doing important service.

This oversight, whether intentional or not, has resulted in some unfortunate side effects. Failing to affirm service outside the structure of the church as also being a service to the Lord has created a negative feeling about the church as a whole and hinders people in experiencing joy in what they give to the church. It has made an unnecessary distinction between the structures of the church and the structures of the world. There are indeed some differences, but great care must be exercised in pointing out both the distinctions and the similarities between these two.

Recognizing these distinctions and similarities leads directly into a deeper discussion of the stewardship of money in support of causes of the church and other worthwhile causes. For instance, the question often is asked, "What all can I include in my tithe? If I support the United Way or the Red Cross, can that money be included in my tithe? Or is my tithe to be given entirely to the church?"

By giving the impression that only the money given to the church directly is what "counts," we make second-rate Christians out of those who give liberally to other causes. Or we at least make them feel that what they give to those causes is not as "holy" as what they give to the church.

Churches have responded in a rather remarkable way to the world hunger crisis. Numerous church bodies have held special financial appeals for world hunger and people have responded generously. Glowing reports have come back from Ethiopia and other African and Asian countries where church relief programs have kept thousands of people alive. Yet churches did not do it alone. Their efforts were coordinated with those of nonchurch agencies, governments, and corporations.

Occasionally, reports of churches to their constituency resort to guilt-producing comments to avoid complacency: "Our church gives only $2 per person to the hunger program a year. That's less than two packages of cigarettes."

True, we all could do more than that and Americans in general do need to reorder their priorities. It may also be true that when we honestly confront the inequities of the world, we rightfully ought to feel guilty. But to leave the impression that our contribution to a churchwide hunger appeal is the only way we work to solve this global problem is to separate church and world too much.

The world hunger problem will not finally be solved by churches having world hunger offerings, although all churches *should* take up world hunger offerings. That not only helps feed people, but also provides impetus for other individuals and agencies to do the same.

Hunger and starvation will finally be conquered when people in the so-called secular occupations of life—farmers, business people, specialists in commerce, scientists, experts in statecraft, diplomats—all plying their daily vocation from Monday through Friday or Saturday, work on production and distribution so that new structures of society will provide more equity.

The talents and resources of people in these areas should be encouraged, and they should be made to feel that they are serving God even if their activities take place outside the structure of the church. Churches sometimes have a special scholarship fund for members going into church occupations. Could the sense of excitement be heightened if scholarships also were offered by congregations to members going into so-called secular vocations that help carry out that first command of God, to care for the earth and its institutions?

When people are affirmed in their daily vocation outside the structure of the church, they also become more excited about supporting the church.

5

THE EFFICIENCY OF STRUCTURE

Those who give to churches have a rightful concern that the money will be used properly and for the projects for which they were intended, without too much being spent on administrative costs.

Administration and *bureaucracy* have almost become dirty words. *Bureaucracy* carries with it the meanings of "excessive multiplication" and "concentration of power" and "red tape," which inhibit the flow of money to the place where it is supposed to accomplish some good. But how much administration is necessary and how much is excessive? Structure is necessary so that money given to the church is used effectively and efficiently. One of the drawbacks of structure is that it can become the end itself rather than a means to an end. When that happens, some of the personal touch between the giver and the receiver is lost. That's why people often say, "I don't want to give to a general national budget; I'd rather give directly to people." But how does one do that?

Three million people swing into action

Let's take a denomination of 5000 congregations with a total membership of 3,000,000 people. An earthquake takes place in a Central American country. Twenty thousand people are killed and many others are left destitute. Christian compassion motivates the 3,000,000 members of that church to want to assist, but how do they go about doing it?

In the first place, how do they find out about the need? And once they have heard about it, where do they send the checks? Furthermore, by the time the checks have arrived, how many additional victims will have died?

Churches are not only appropriate institutions through which help can be sent, but they have a recognized record of doing so effectively and at low cost. Structures and administration are simply the methods by which resources are gathered and moved expeditiously to the place where they can effectively do the work that needs to be done.

So the first step is getting word to the 5000 congregations about the need and explaining procedure of where to send funds and how they will be used. Getting the money together and sending it to the place of need may absorb as much as 5 or 10 or 15 percent of the total, but the amount spent for this (administrative) cost is no less holy than the amount actually used to help the victims. In fact, without this 5, 10, or 15 percent devoted to administrative cost, the 85, 90, or 95 percent would not have been raised to provide help to those in need.

This is not just a hypothetical case. An earthquake actually took place in Guatemala some years ago. And because that church had an administrative structure and a general treasury, it was able immediately to send $50,000 to the victims, as well as a planeload of clothing, food, and medical supplies, before it even sent out the request for help to its members.

Helping the earthquake victims was not the only project in which these 5000 congregations were engaged in the course of that year. In fact, that was a relatively small part of its annual program. If each part of the denomination's program had its own separate administrative budget for raising and distributing money, there would have been a lot of duplication. So this denomination has a national office through which money is raised for all of those programs. While people may get a special thrill out of being able to point to precise activities accomplished with the dollars they gave, they also should get a thrill out of supporting a structure so efficient that it can swing into action immediately to meet emergency needs, as well as long-term programs.

Necessary but not glamorous

A second reason for contributing to a general treasury is that it makes possible the necessary projects that might not be supported because they lack glamour.

For example: Since overseas mission continues to have an appeal, let's say that a congregation sends $1000 to its denominational office and says, "We want this money used directly and only for overseas missions." How would the church use that money to abide by the request of the congregation?

Well, how does a church body decide where to send missionaries in the first place? It certainly doesn't flip a coin to decide between Asia and Africa.

That thousand dollars might be used to send a skilled mission executive to various countries to explore the challenges and needs. Without this basic background study, there would be no mission to support.

Suppose now that a decision has been made to start a mission station in Africa. Where does a missionary come from? It is not likely that a person will walk in off the street some Wednesday morning and say, "I want to be a missionary." That happens occasionally, but not often enough for a church to build a long-range program of missionary recruitment on such occurrences.

It may well be that a 12-year-old boy or girl read a story about a missionary in a Sunday school paper that kindled the desire to be a missionary. That story did not appear by accident. It was probably part of a long-range plan of the church to develop a cadre of missionaries. It is not likely, however, that the congregation would have requested that their $1000 be used to underwrite the printing costs of that kind of a publication. It just doesn't sound very glamorous. Yet without a recruitment program, there eventually would be no missionaries to send overseas.

Now, let's say that a half dozen or so young men and women, 18 years old, are deeply interested in overseas mission work. They need an education and special training. The mission board could, of course, sponsor special training programs for missionaries. Would the congregation accept their $1000 being spent for the education of missionaries as an appropriate use of their funds? Or would they insist that it actually be used in a country where the missionaries are at work? Without the former, the latter would not be possible.

Or, instead of developing a program of missionary training of its own, the mission board might say, "Our church already operates colleges and seminaries where these young people can be trained. May we use the $1000 to support one of our church's colleges?"

These questions are raised to illustrate that the various programs of the church are interrelated. Not all of them have an equal appeal. If only those that are especially appealing were funded, other equally important parts of the program might not be funded. And then even the appealing ones could not be done.

In the illustration of a congregation wanting to give $1000 to send a missionary to an African country, that amount obviously is not enough to pay all of the expense involved. So, where does the rest of the money come from? It comes from people who have contributed to the general treasury of the national church. Or, suppose that one congregation did indeed make a contribution large enough to pay all of the expenses for sending a missionary family to Africa. What would happen if the following year that congregation decided to sponsor a missionary in Asia? Would the family that had been sponsored the year before have to be brought back home again? Very likely, that family would continue in Africa, but would be supported by funds given to the general treasury.

Another project that enjoys a lot of popular appeal these days is world hunger. The media has helped us see the tremendous size of this problem. It is hard to forget the pictures of sad eyes, gaunt faces, and bloated stomachs of children who go to bed hungry every night. There is a natural and compasssionate response to want to help.

But how can money given to world hunger be used best? There is an old saying: "Give a man a fish and you feed him for a day, but teach him how to fish and you make it possible for him to feed himself for many days." Many people, however, seem to find greater satisfaction in knowing that the money they gave actually paid for food that was given to a hungry person. Using money to teach people good habits and nutrition does not seem to have as much appeal, and yet that use probably would result in more effective feeding of people.

At times, it may even be proper to use money given to alleviate hunger to build roads or bridges or boats. If, for instance, people are starving in one part of a country, but there is ample food in another part, the problem may be a lack of transportation facilities to get the food to where the hungry people are. Making that transportation possible actually results in bringing food to those who are starving.

A third part to that lesson, "Give a man a fish or teach him how to fish," is often forgotten. What happens if the laws or government of a country deny people of a certain color or from certain ethnic or economic groups a place on the stream from where they can fish? What happens if all the land is owned by a few people and the great majority are prevented from getting land? It is acceptable to send agriculturalists to Third World countries to teach methods of agriculture. Is it equally acceptable to send political scientists to assist the people in restructuring an oppressive government?

These illustrations have been used to support the value of having an organized structure with a staff to develop programs to make sure that all the elements of a program are supported. This support comes from a general budget, rather than depending on the moods of individuals who might want to support this or that program, but who lack an overall view of the whole ministry of the church.

Admittedly, there are times when giving to a general budget does not engender quite the enthusiasm one might get from giving to specific causes. This simply increases the challenge for church communicators to point out how support of the general budget does indeed accomplish some very exciting things.

The obvious solution is that it need not be an either/or situation—either all contributions given to the national budget or all given to individual, special causes. There can be joy and excitement in both approaches and ways of giving.

The case has been made for the efficiency of structure and of a general budget to support that structure. The next part of the book will make the case for support of special causes.

6

THE CASE FOR GIVING TO SPECIAL CAUSES

The first five chapters have been somewhat traditional, theological, and theoretical: traditional, in that they followed a recognized stewardship education approach of emphasizing the motivation for giving as a response to the love of God; theological, in that they put stewardship in a larger context of a relationship to God in all that we have and do; theoretical, in that we began with theory and theology as the basis for the practical.

Psychologists tell us that learning does not always take place by going from theory to practice. Sometimes it happens in reverse. You begin by doing something without regard to theory, but the action is so satisfying that it substantiates a theory, which then not only gives all the more incentive for action, but also for going more deeply into the theory.

For instance, one person commenting on the concept of excitement or guilt said, "When one is first committed to serving the Lord, then and *only then* can money produce excitement and not guilt for the Christian." Granted the normal flow of events for the Christian is commitment first and then a response based on that commitment. But let's not limit the ways God leads people. People may find joy and excitement in supporting a Christian cause and then, as a result, come to a deeper knowledge of Christ and a commitment to him.

A gift from the Third World

We have the churches of the Third World and, particularly, liberation theology to thank for some new insights. Perhaps the biggest contribution to us has been a wider vision of the various ways in which God works; God can work from practice to theory (or theology), as well as from theory (or theology) to practice.

Liberation theology has been much abused by people having a meager understanding of it, who immediately associate it with communism or see it as turning the gospel into a political theory.

Traditional and classical theology has served us well and should not be discarded. But it is not the only way to view or explain God's action in the world. Most American clergy received their theological training in the classroom. In the safety of the classroom one can study how God's people have been led through the centuries. The Old Testament is rife with marvelous stories, including God's creation of the universe and God's covenant with the people of Israel. The New Testament holds similar excitement in the teachings of Jesus, the travels and letters of Paul, and the messages of the Gospels.

To get added insights, theological students work through the original languages in which the Bible was written, Hebrew and Greek, and study the culture of biblical times so they can understand the message of the Bible even better. They develop skills in preaching and counseling and parish administration. All of this is done in the classroom to provide a good theoretical basis.

This approach has resulted in a church program throughout the world that has indeed made the gospel meaningful to people. It has provided a good, thorough basis for church extension and growth in all parts of the world. Social service agencies have been formed to bring healing to people who have been hurt, either by their own folly or by forces of injustices.

But that is not the only way that God works. In fact, the 12 disciples might not have been accepted by many of the church's best theological seminaries. The young churches of the developing world have helped us recapture some of the power of the gospel and convinced us that the gospel is more than an abstract or theological theory. It actually works in life.

One of the chief messages of the Old Testament is the story of the Exodus. God heard the people's cry of anguish and bondage and delivered them. Today's oppressed people have taken new heart that God will hear them in their bondage and oppression. God indeed is not dependent on a fully accredited theological education program to get things done. This in no way denigrates a classical theological education, but only serves as a reminder that God works in various ways. Perhaps we can learn something using this approach in the realm of stewardship education too.

Enthusiasm versus realism

One reason stewardship performance in the area of money given to the church is often lacking may be linked to a dogged refusal—at least on the part of some—that action can precede theory. Church stewardship programs can be so insistent that the right motivation must be present before giving is acceptable that the givers feel guilty if they experience joy by giving from other motivations. Thus further giving is stifled. One national church executive often referred to money given outside of the national budget of his church body as "bootleg" giving.

The consideration of the budget at national church conventions often paves the way for some self-fulfilling prophecies. One would think that national executives, who know the needs well and have a deep passion for wanting the church to meet those needs, would recommend challenging budgets. But their definition of challenge is often far less than that of the delegates.

So, the budget proposal comes in with the recommendation of a three or four percent increase over the previous year's budget or, at times, as high as a 10 percent increase. Delegates think this is an insult. They quickly engage in some mathematics and conclude that that would come to three or four milkshakes or movies or a pack of cigarettes a year per person. "And *that* you call a challenge," they say in an almost sneering fashion.

But the fiscal officers are also realistic. They have heard these speeches before and have a record of what these speeches have produced over the past decade or so, an increase of about four or five percent a year. No matter how high the enthusiasm for a 10 or 15 percent increase may be, fiscal officers know they must be responsible and accountable for their actions. What would happen if the church, based on the enthusiasm of delegates' promises, would adopt a budget of 15 percent above last year's budget and initiate programs on that basis, only to have to cut them back at the end of the year?

The tension between realism and enthusiasm is necessary. One reason realism wins out is the assumption that the same methods of stewardship education that have been used in the past will continue to be used. And, of course, they bring the same results, about a four or five percent increase, usually not enough to keep up with inflation. It is based on the assumption that the theory-to-practice approach is the best, if not the only, way to go.

People usually concede that the theory-to-practice approach hasn't worked in the past. So a special appeal is called for and approved, with a strong stipulation, however, that it *not* be called a fund appeal. It must be called stewardship education. To make the appeal even stronger, it must incorporate a *biblical* approach to stewardship.

But may it be that even a biblical approach to stewardship is too narrow, if it allows for only one approach?

The Bible itself may allow for much broader interpretations, ones more exciting than have been used in the past.

Several of these already have been described. Giving out of a thankful heart to the God who has first given to us is indeed a powerful motivation—perhaps even the best motivation—for good stewardship. But so are several others that the church may approve in theory but seldom promote with great enthusiasm.

There was a time when the church stated that properly motivated stewards do not give because of the appeal of special causes. Allowance was made for those who, in spite of everything, insisted on giving to special causes. But it was often with a kind of grumbling attitude that said, "Well, we wish you would give for the right reason. But if you insist on giving to special causes, we'll take it."

The point is that no *one* way is the *only* way to support the budget of the church—such as having a well-organized structure to carry out a systematic program, which in turn necessitates a general treasury. Most of the logic may well be on that side. But the assumption that everything in life operates logically needs to be questioned. The actions of God cannot be explained by logic either.

What kind of logic is there, for instance, in having a walk-a-thon or a bike-a-thon or a Hands Across America project in which people are paid for every mile they walk or ride or $10 just for holding hands? What good does the walking or the riding or the handholding do? Wouldn't it be just as easy simply to give the money without the nonproductive activity? Logic would say so. But life is made up of more than logic. Some actions are symbolic, and participating in the symbols can bring joy in itself. People ought not be denied that joy. The very participation can add to insight and thus feed back into strengthened theory and theology.

Many congregations have struggled and disagreed over the appropriateness of bake sales, bazaars, and car washes as an acceptable way of raising money for the church. A distinction is made between money raising and "pure" stewardship.

An insistence on total purity of stewardship motivation can be nonproductive if too much energy is devoted to the battle of whether or not to have money-raising events in the church. To be sure, if the event is sponsored purely for the sake of raising money, without any consideration of other values that might come from it, then a good argument can be made against it. But the events generally do have some good side benefits. The opportunity for getting together with people of the community is not to be underrated in an era when there is far too little attention given to such relationships.

Furthermore, some people simply do not have incomes to make even small contributions to the church, and yet they desperately want to make a contribution. They do get a good feeling out of using their own flour and butter and sugar to bake a cake, which can then be sold for more than what the ingredients cost. Why deny older people the joy of feeling they can contribute by spending hours—of which they have plenty—doing needlework or some other craft, which can be sold and the proceeds given to the church?

Both sides need rethinking

Those who have been elected to executive positions in the church need not lower their commitment to responsible and logical reasoning as they plan programs. They have a high calling. The Holy Spirit does not work in a vacuum. One need not speak of ecclesiastical machinery in snide tones. Even church "politics" ought not to be a bad term. Machinery and politics are simply the methods by which things are accomplished—to be sure by sinful, fallible human beings, but under the guidance of the Holy Spirit.

The democratic process by which boards are elected, committees appointed, and programs planned is not less spiritual because these actions are accomplished by human beings whose motives at times may not be entirely selfless. After all, if even the best of us feel the need for daily confession of sin—and on Sundays we do it in public before a full congregation of people—why should it be surprising if decisions made in regard to the church's work are more tainted by the human than by the divine? The checks and balances inherent in the democratic process may well be the way the Holy Spirit operates in the church.

Elected church officials, who through the democratic process plan church programs, have every right to expect the respect and prayers of the members. They have to make some difficult decisions. What are the correct priorities? Should they use a given amount of money—the national budget, if you will—to build a new college or to start 10 new congregations? People equally spiritual and equally intelligent may arrive at different conclusions. But even after the decision is made not to start a new congregation here or a mission station there or to develop an expensive television program, God may lay it on the heart of someone to make a sizable gift to do precisely that. Should that person be criticized for challenging the decision made by church authorities? History could prove that the action of the individual was unwise. It also could prove that the action of the church officials was unwise.

Many a mission project that is quite successful today was started by a few individuals, sometimes in opposition to official decisions of the church, and was later taken over by the church. Perhaps an equal number of projects started against church opposition would have been better served had they not been started. Sometimes, perhaps even most of the time, God speaks through the majority. Sometimes, however, God speaks through the minority.

Simply being in the minority is no assurance that God is on one's side. There can be a tendency of those who bypass official church action and programs and start independent projects to call into question the wisdom or even the Christian dedication of those elected to church positions. A minority can be as arrogant as a majority.

But what does all of this have to do with the stewardship of money? God works in a variety of ways to accomplish the divine will. God works through structures of the organized church and blesses its efforts. Human structures can become divine channels. Supporting the budget of a national church body can be exciting when it is clear that that is one way God's will is accomplished.

Whatever its original intention may have been, 1 Corinthians 12 illustrates how all the parts of the body work together. Some seem important, others not so important. But they all serve the body. Some parts of a national church program seem more important and a little more exciting. Others serve as a foundation, not seen, but without them the structure would collapse.

Had Paul gone into greater medical and anatomical detail in his letter to the Corinthians, he might have referred to some parts of the body that are a total mystery as to how they relate to the whole and what function they serve.

The analogy doesn't quite hold up all the way, because as long as human beings are fallible there will be some programs—whether designed by the institutional church or by independent, spiritual entrepreneurs—that are, quite frankly, the work of Satan. It is always easy to jump to the conclusion that those designed by the other person fall in that category. The conviction that we are called by God to do what we do must combine assurance with humility.

7

WAYS TO GROW IN STEWARDSHIP

This chapter might be entitled, "Things You've Thought About Stewardship But Were Afraid to Ask." Included will be some ideas that individuals or churches have tried. Some are more distantly related to stewardship, but serve to stretch the mind, so as to look at the whole subject from a different point of view.

First, let us consider some statistical facts about the population in general and about the church population. Do some age-groups give more than others? How much do they give? What kinds of projects do they support?

A national survey on "The Charitable Behavior of Americans" was conducted recently by Yankelovich, Skelly and White, Inc., commissioned by The Rockefeller Brothers Fund.*

The fact that these findings report what the giving behavior of Americans is does not mean that churches should make their stewardship efforts conform to this behavior or even use these findings to manipulate people into giving. However, the findings may give a better understanding of people and their giving habits. Then, if there is to be stewardship education, churches will at least know where to begin and with whom.

The research shows that 89 percent of Americans reported giving to charities in 1984. Eleven percent gave between $1 and $50; 11 percent gave between $50 and

---

*The findings have been published in two brief volumes totaling 66 pages and are available from Independent Sector, 1828 L Street, NW, Washington, D.C. 20036. This complete report will be helpful to anyone conducting fund-raising and stewardship education programs.

$100; 18 percent gave between $100 and $250; 13 percent gave between $250 and $500; 13 percent gave between $500 and $1000; 10 percent gave between $1000 and $2000; and 8 percent contributed more than $2000. One-third of all Americans gave $500 or more to religious and other charities in 1984.

The average annual contribution of those 89 percent who did give to charitable causes was $740. Americans gave an average of 2.4 percent of their household incomes to charities in 1984. While more than half of all Americans gave less than one percent of their income to charities, more than 25 percent gave 3 percent of their incomes to charities. Thirteen percent gave 5 percent or more of their income to charity. Approximately 70 percent of individual giving went to religious causes.

There is a clear relationship between regular attendance at religious services and giving to religious charities. Average total contributions for those who attended religious services weekly was more than three times as great ($990) as for those who did not attend at all ($300). Those who pledged a certain dollar amount each week to their church gave an average of almost twice as much ($880) to religious charities as did those who did not pledge ($460).

The survey also found a strong relationship between volunteering and giving. Of the 26 percent of the general population who fell into the "substantial giver" category (those contributing more than 3 percent of their annual income) nearly three out of five said they were active as volunteers.

One of the factors that influences giving is the amount of discretionary income people feel they have. An interesting finding of the survey was that among people with moderate discretionary income, 25 percent of those under 35 are substantial givers (giving more than 3 percent of their income) while 40 per cent of those over 35 are in this category.

Although the impact that religion has on giving is not clear-cut, the study did find that religious beliefs motivated giving to causes in the following order: charities that assist the poor, organizations that help needy people in other countries, medical charities, and educational institutions.

The kinds of nonchurch organizations most likely to be supported are (in order of choice): United Way, medical charities (heart, cancer, etc.), local social welfare groups (Scouts, etc), international relief and assistance, colleges and universities, public radio and television, hospitals, environmental groups, and others (art groups, libraries, other educational charities, etc.).

But the largest contributions in order of choice were to colleges, educational charity, United Way, hospitals, local social-welfare groups, and medical charities.

Another finding of the study was that, especially for big gifts, people are most likely to respond to direct requests from an individual they know.

Tithing—relationship versus percentage

Make no mistake about it, tithing has to do with percentage. And the figure is 10 percent. Why then all the debate? Doesn't the Bible say a person should give 10 percent of everything to God? (In a superficial translation we say that means 10 percent to the church, although in Chapter 4 that was broadened somewhat to include activities of nonchurch organizations.) But can we rationalize away the 10 percent as being too legalistic, or even enhance it be saying that 10 percent ought to be a *beginning* point?

This is one of those areas that illustrates the idolatry of certainty. Let me digress. The Bible has very little to say about atheism, except perhaps for Psalm 14: "The fool says in his heart, 'There is no God.' "

For the Old Testament, particularly, the question is not, "Is there a God or is there not a God?" The question is, "Is there one God, or are their many gods, and what is the characteristic that distinguishes the one true God from the false gods?" The question is one of idolatry, not atheism.

One major characteristic of the true God is God's otherworldly nature. God placed Moses in a cleft in a rock and walked past; Moses could look on God's back and accept in faith that it was God.

Human beings like proof, something that can be seen, touched, counted. We prefer proof to trust. But a relationship with God is built on trust, not proof. That is why a reliance on proof for certainty is idolatry.

In relationship to the tithe, 10 percent is something we can count. It is quite precise. We can point to it. Yet when we give greater attention to the amount than to the principle behind the amount, then we are guilty of idolatry. True, many people try to wiggle out from under the seeming enormity of the 10 percent by calling it legalism. But what they are really trying to escape is the relationship for which that tithe stands.

For the faithful Old Testament Israelites the tithe served as a monumental reminder of who they were and whose they were. They belonged to God. Everything that they had belonged to God and came from God. They were stewards and trustees. Ten percent had nothing to do with the thought that this amount belonged to God and the rest they could use as they pleased, or even that they had to use the rest to please God too. The chief thing was the relationship.

How could that be anything but exciting? Why turn it into guilt? An appeal to tithing as a means for raising more money, along with the ensuing debate about whether the 10 percent ought to be of the gross or the net, is all beside the point.

A man with an income of a million dollars might well give 10 percent or 20 or 30 percent of that to a worthy cause and still not have done so with any spirit of the tithe. A church may convince some of its wealthy members to give 10 percent of their income to the church and still not have performed a ministry for them.

To be sure, there is nothing wrong with a church urging people to tithe and thereby increase the money with which it can do God-pleasing things. But if in so doing the people have not caught the spirit of the tithe, the realization that they belong to God and that all they have comes from God, they may still be giving out of guilt and not experience excitement.

Here, too, we see that learning does not always follow in a direct line from theory and theology to practice. Sometimes it can go in reverse order. Some people may be inspired to give large sums of money—a single, double, or triple tithe—just because it makes them feel good. They should not be made to bear the guilt of being told that they are giving it for the wrong reason. (The church that received such a gift probably wouldn't think of being anything but happy for the occasion.) But the church has a greater ministry of increasing the excitement by helping the donors see their relationship to God.

Creative ways of building relationships

Creativity can get out of hand at times. There are ways of doing things that seem appropriate for the church and others that don't; and sometimes the line between them is rather thin. There's good reason, therefore, for some rules and regulations. We have already stated the case for the efficiency and necessity of structure. On the whole these are good.

The problem comes when a new idea is brought before a review committee. Many of the idea's weaknesses are spotted immediately and the idea is thrown out because it doesn't fit the structure or is too difficult to implement. That may be one reason why the stewardship of mainline churches stays quite constant. The sizable increases in giving happen in groups that are open to innovative ideas.

Mainline churches have made some progress in this area by allowing and even encouraging special gifts and yoking arrangements. While there may be a national budget through which most of the money flows, groups of congregations are also encouraged to support special projects directly and thus establish a personal relationship. The same is the case in supporting overseas missionaries. While much or even most of the support for a missionary may still come through a national budget, individual congregations are urged to adopt a missionary as their own, perhaps even to list him or her on the congregational letterhead as its overseas missionary. Some support the Missionary-for-a-Day project, in which the total annual support of a missionary is prorated on a daily basis, and a congregation agrees to pick up the cost for one day.

The problem with these arrangements is that they sometimes carry the stigma of falling short of the way gifts ought to be. It is, as it were, a concession to a less desirable way of doing things. There is the problem of accounting for these gifts. Are they a part of the congregation's regular benevolence, or are they extras (as though the regular benevolence were more acceptable than the extra)?

There is the reasonable fear that if a church were to go all out in support of these extras, the contributions to the regular program might suffer.

One of the more creative ways of building relationships on a global basis is the "yoking map" proposed by John and Sylvia Ronsvalle, in their book *The Hidden Billions, the Potential of the Church in the U.S.A.* The Ronsvalles direct an organization in Urbana, Illinois, known as The Empty Tomb, Inc.

The Empty Tomb has designed a comprehensive map, yoking every county in the United States with an area in a foreign country and developing a relationship with the people and the churches there.

The Ronsvalles suggest a 60-20-20 program:

> **Perhaps current church giving is below 10 percent because many church members are not effectively challenged by the vision of the church. How often have we heard the comment that increased giving to the church will only result in bigger buildings, a newer organ, or more staff.**
>
> **This problem may be a matter of pot and kettle calling each other names: church staff may claim members are challenged only by organ funds and something on which they can put a plaque, while church members may complain the contributed money would not make it to missions.**

The Ronsvalles point out that contributions to the church is currently at the 1.6 percent level. An average of 80 percent of that stays within the congregation:

> **If giving were to increase to 10 percent, self-discipline could be used within the congregation to use only 20 percent within the local church. Then 60 percent could go for overseas missions and an additional 20 percent could go for mission and denominational expenses within the U.S.**

Undoubtedly, there may be several or even many snags in the suggestions made by the Ronsvalles. But that kind of creative thinking ought to be encouraged. Members of congregations ought to be challenged to do some creative thinking and their suggestions ought to be seriously considered. That is not to say that they would be without flaw or that they should be accepted lock, stock, and barrel. But the first response from a national stewardship board ought not be, "That won't work."

Growth giving

One American denomination, The American Lutheran Church, has designed a program called Growth Giving. The explanation for it is a bit complex. But the theory is good, and with some modifications it could lead the way to a program as exciting as that recommended by the Ronsvalles.

Growth Giving calls for a 1-percent increase of total income given to the church each year by every member, and for a 1-percent increase of the total congregational budget devoted to benevolence each year. This is a bit tricky to explain. It does not mean that you increase your giving by 1 percent over last year, so that if you gave $1000 last year you will give $1010 this year. It means that if you gave 2 percent of your total income last year you will give 3 percent of your total this year, 4 percent next year, and 5 percent the following year. Last year the $1000 would have been 2 percent of a total income of $50,000. This year it would be 3 percent or $1500; next year it would be 4 percent or $2000, etc. In the meantime, of course, one's salary would probably have gone up also, so the increased percent would have been on the higher salary.

In the same way, if a church gave 10 percent of its total budget to benevolence this year, it would give 11 percent next year, and 12 percent the following year. In a church body with 5000 congregations, this could mean millions of dollars increase for national and global programs within several years.

One problem with the interpretation of such a plan is that it can easily become a structure-and-budget story rather than a story that relates people to people. The two are not mutually exclusive. A structure-and-budget story can be told in terms of how it reaches people, but it takes special skill to do so. Even when the attempt is to tell people stories, the final product still sometimes ends up telling structure-and-budget stories.

Willingness to take risks

People who are used to thinking in terms of investing know the meaning of risk and are excited by it. Risk does not mean recklessness. It involves careful, rational thought and decision making, weighing the odds of success and failure. But in the business world, many investments are made even though the certainty of success is far less than 100 percent. There will undoubtedly be some failures, which should be taken in stride.

One needs to be careful, of course, about whose money is being risked, one's own or someone else's. When persons freely give contributions to the church, that money is no longer their own. They have given it to the church and entrusted the officials of the church with the responsible use of that money. The church officials should be willing to risk a certain amount of that money for projects that do not have a 100 percent guarantee of safety, success, or quick return.

They may decide, for instance, to invest money in starting a new congregation in an area where perhaps only two or three of the usual five or six indicators for successful growth are present. It may well become obvious after a few years that the decision was not the best. But don't write it off too quickly as a failure. It may be that several people were influenced by the mission who later turn out to be giants in the church and in society.

As with financial investments, there needs to be a "balanced portfolio," some projects that are virtually risk-free and others that have some risk. During the '60s and '70s the church often was accused of playing everything "too safe." It was accused of starting missions only in the rapidly growing suburbs, where it was difficult if not impossible to fail. New congregations could become self-supporting in three years or less.

When the same expectations were laid on congregations being started in the inner city, they didn't work out. It needs to be kept in mind, however, that often it is those congregations that grow rapidly and achieve self-support that are willing to provide the finances that make it possible to start other congregations that need financial support for a longer period of time.

It is not quite fair to blame the church for *never* taking risks. Equally committed people may differ in their opinion as to whether the "mix" is correct, whether the "portfolio" is balanced or not. A certain amount of healthy risk adds excitement to the work of the church, for God is often a God of surprises. True, most of the time, the ways of God may be very similar to the ways of human beings, for God works through human beings. But what a tragedy it is if opportunities are not allowed for the breakthrough of some divine surprises.

Again, care should be used in investing other people's money. At times the church acts as a trustee for other people's money. Pension funds are a prime example. Because denominational pension funds are huge in size, they become an easy target for people in search for funds for worthwhile causes. These people make a good case that the church, of all institutions, ought to be willing to take some risks and thereby give a powerful witness to the world in the way it invests its money. It's as simple as the saying, "Put your money where your mouth is." If the church really wants to make an impact, then it should be willing to risk its money for projects that will help people even though the returns may not be equal to what other investments might bring.

The only problem with that argument is that the pension fund does not belong to the church; it belongs to people. And the church (in this case, the investment committee) has been entrusted with the task of investing it in the most prudent manner that will bring the highest return for the least amount of risk.

There continues to be a tension between conservatively oriented fiscal officers and social-action oriented members of the church. There are indeed legal restraints on the ways pension money can be invested, which social activists do not always appreciate. There can, however, also be an unwillingness on the part of the church's fiscal officers to take an objective look at new approaches to investment. The debate between the two views can be wholesome, adding to the excitement that is always present when new, creative ways are found in which money can carry out God's work in the world.

Enlarging the pie or simply recutting it

One reason there is often a shortage of money in church budgets—national, regional, district, or congregational—is that these budgets are put together by human beings who are not perfect. For the most part, they are honestly and deeply committed to the causes they represent and are convinced that their department's work is important to the kingdom. After all, they have been elected or appointed by the church to be the director of a specific department and have the welfare of that department at heart. They would not be fulfilling their duty if they did not speak up for their causes in the annual budget discussions.

The annual debate in the budget committee or on the convention floor is predictable. A request comes in for an increased allocation for one of the departments, and the immediate question is, "Which department is willing to give up some of its allocation so that the request can be honored?" There is seldom any question about the importance of the new proposal. The question always is, "Which is *more* important?"

Administrative structures often have difficulty dealing with this impasse. There is a strong emphasis on the autonomy of individual departments, but who has the authority to decide between departments? Once a percentage has been decided upon as an appropriate division among various departments, must that percentage remain fixed forever after? It's the old question, "How do you cut the pie?" How can a bigger piece be given to one without giving a smaller piece to someone else?

One answer, of course, is to enlarge the pie. Experience has taught, however, that that seldom happens, at least as long as the same methods are used in gathering funds. To be sure, there usually is an annual increase in contributions to the church, but that increase often is the result of inflation and barely takes care of, or does not take care of, inflation. So, we're back to the old problem of recutting the pie in different-sized pieces. This annual exercise, or the call for that exercise, is not all bad, though. It forces a congregation to rethink its priorities; that is always wholesome, even though it may be painful.

As is often the case, the answer is not an either/or decision. A both/and approach is far more exciting. In fact, a greater willingness to consider recutting the pie into different-sized pieces may exhibit the kind of loyalty to the church's ministry that inspires people to want to enlarge the pie.

New type of reporting

As simple an approach as finding different ways of reporting could add new zest to giving to or investing in the work of the church, thus adding to a "larger pie."

I do not want to belittle the tendency of church executives, particularly those in charge of financial affairs, to develop a technical language of their own. Accounting is important and, when the sums are large, becomes all the more important. Certain accounts need to be kept separate and distinct; and each of these accounts must be identified. Added to this is the insistence of congregational members to know how their money is used. The task is not easy.

A communication problem also exists. Communication is a two-way street. There is a message-sender and a message-receiver. For the two to understand each other they have to use the same words. But who decides what words are to be used? Since the sender originates the message, he or she usually decides what words should be used and then assumes or insists that the receiver use the same language. Senders often insist that the receivers put themselves in the senders' shoes rather than the senders putting themselves in the receivers' shoes.

A good name for this communication approach is "administrative thinking." It is important, or at least useful, for church executives to have a clear understanding of the mission and objectives of the church. And ever since the days of management by objective, these objectives have been described in specific, technical terms that have meaning for church executives and help them define their tasks.

Interpretive pieces designed by church communication offices often tell the budget-and-structure story. This department does this and spends this amount of money; that department does that and spends that amount of money. This type of reporting stems from the assumption (usually correct) that people want to know how their money is spent. The information given in this way is important, factual, and about as exciting as an encyclopedia.

Are there, perhaps, other ways to communicate this message, ways that are more exciting? Simply changing the medium and going from black-and-white print to four-color printing on glossy paper with a lot of pictures is not enough. Nor is the problem solved by giving the same kind of information, but doing it through films, videotape, or television.

There's a need for a new way of telling the church story. One of the most exciting parts about that task is that in a church body of 3,000,000 members there are 3,000,000 people to help tell the story. Every church member has a story to tell. Part of the task of a communication office is to help these 3,000,000 members experience what the church means to them and to show how *they* can tell that story.

One of the glories and excitement of the Christian faith is the fact that at the foot of the cross all people are equal. The day laborer with a minimum income may have much in common with the town millionaire. They may both have experienced the death of a spouse or a son or a daughter, and in an evening of storytelling they might find a new excitement in sharing their faith.

Be open to the surprises that may come as people from all walks of life in the congregation share their personal stories. Some congregations have initiated storytelling events and are finding them an exhilarating experience. One need not—in fact, should not—take up an offering for the church at each of these events. The experiences, however, do tend to sow seeds that sprout and grow and sometimes produce fruit a hundredfold, even in terms of dollars, to say nothing of a renewed appreciation for the joy of Christian living.

8

TEN IDEAS FOR DISCUSSION

No matter how good a theory may be, there comes a time when you have to get practical and outline a detailed plan of action. Your church is now planning its annual stewardship emphasis, and you have been named to the committee to help plan it. Now come some very practical questions. Should you have an every-member visit? Should you have a series of dinners or gatherings in homes? How many callers will you need? How will you arrive at your goal?

These are all important questions. They will not be addressed in this chapter, however, because they are generally known. Congregations have been through these procedure before, and there are many helps available to guide them through these steps. What often is lacking is the in-between step of generating a number of ideas, questions, or general principles regarding stewardship from tradition, theology, and theory. A brainstorming session can help to clarify steps that a congregation, its pastor, and committee members might take in its year-round emphasis on the stewardship of money.

1. While nine out of ten people interviewed in a national survey made a contribution to the church or some charitable cause, nearly 40 percent felt they ought to have given more. They felt guilty. This fact underscores the opportunity and challenge for stewardship motivation. Maybe one reason we feel guilty is that we *are* guilty. Often our priorities are wrong. My argument, however, is that excitement may be a better motivation than guilt. If people already feel guilt, it is questionable

whether the church ought to add to that guilt. Without just sweeping guilt under the rug, how does one talk about it? One suggestion is to place more emphasis on the excitement that comes from investing.

This is a difficult subject for many to talk about in a one-on-one conversation, particularly for a pastor with individual members of the congregation. One reason for this might be precisely because this conversation so often has taken place in a context of guilt. It is not enough to say to somebody, "You ought to be excited about this." Excitement is engendered through personal experience or through the stories of what others have experienced. A pastor might give a copy of this book to someone with whom he or she would like to discuss the stewardship of money, and simply say, "I'd like to talk to you about this sometime. I'd like your opinion about some of the things in this book."

2. The below-35 age group was identified as being below average in giving, even though they had considerable discretionary funds. A special stewardship education approach might be designed for this group. A beginning discussion might include them in order to understand what their particular problems, feelings, and insights might be. The investment concept might be most appealing to the below-35 age group because many of them are in the midst of thinking through their own investments. Furthermore, this age group is a crucial one for leadership development and for the future of the church. This group might be a key group to challenge with the discipline of Growth Giving, as described in Chapter 7.

3. The Rockefeller study confirms with data what most of us intuitively feel, that by far the best givers to religious causes are those who go to church regularly. This does not mean that we should strive for large church attendance simply to increase financial support. It does suggest, however, that one of the by-products

of increased church attendance is increased offerings. The main reason for worship is to experience something of the awe and mystery of standing before God and being accepted through grace.

4. The Rockefeller study also substantiated the assumption that people who volunteer are more likely to contribute financially. The church, therefore, needs to be creative in finding meaningful volunteer assignments in which people can use their skills and abilities. Ushering, singing in the choir, serving on committees, teaching Sunday school are all important volunteer tasks that should not be underrated. However, they are not the *only* tasks that can involve people. One way to be more innovative might be to bring together a number of members and ask *them* for creative ways in which they would like to be involved.

5. Take advantage of where people are in their everyday life. Many of them understand the concepts of trusteeship and investing. In the business world people are responsible for money that is not theirs, thus providing an excellent basis for an emphasis on stewardship. Let that understanding become the basis for reminding them that everything they have has been loaned them by God. Not everything in the business world translates directly into the church, and there is a danger that business people may forget that fact when they are placed on church boards. A successful business is successful partly because it continually tries to work with the best in quality, particularly in the employees it hires. The church is much more attuned to being deeply interested in everyone, even the "losers" in life. The two are not mutually exclusive. A church might at times be better off if it learned from business how to turn losers into winners. Business executives should be grateful for the fact that the church has deep compassion for losers, for they may one day find themselves in a situation where they too desperately need the compassion the

church has to offer. The two groups need to be in constant dialog with each other. Business people can bring their expertise to the management of church affairs and be ministered to through the pastoral skills of the church.

6. Don't be afraid to talk about tithing or the definition of tithing as giving 10 percent of one's income. But above all, don't overlook the purpose of the tithe. If that is emphasized, the arithmetic will take care of itself. The tithe serves as a powerful reminder of the relationship with God, the giver of all that we have. The icing on the cake is the excitement that comes from investing that tithe and seeing it become productive.

7. Church structures need to be flexibile when developing programs for ministry and to take into account people's natural interest in worthwhile causes. For instance, the national survey discovered the high priority people give to educational institutions and programs that assist the poor and needy. While there may be a danger of proliferating the specific causes for which financial appeals are conducted, there is also a danger of so jealously guarding the general treasury and budget of the church that people's natural inclination to support the church is stifled. The system imposed on them may seem to denigrate certain forms of giving. Studies indicate that giving begets giving. If an intelligent and interesting case is made for general programs, as well as for specific programs, people will support a balanced program.

8. Don't be afraid of an appropriate mechanism that highlights specific causes. One may question the logic of walk-a-thons, bike-a-thons, and Hands Across America as ways of raising money. What good does it do to agree to pay a young person a specific amount of money for every mile that he or she walks or rides a bike? Why not just contribute the money directly to the

worthwhile project and thus maintain the "purity" of stewardship theology? There is another part of that logic, however, that must be remembered, and that is that these activities serve an educational and bonding purpose. The activity highlights the cause and brings about a clearer understanding of its purpose. It also bonds people together in common cause.

9. Churches need to tell the story of their work in interesting and exciting ways. This requires a balance of information and inspiration, of the cognitive and the affective. A certain amount of cognitive information is important so that people can see that something worthwhile is being accomplished, but it usually is not very inspiring. Stories of people are necessary, stories of people whose lives have been touched by the gospel through the church. People are much more likely to invest in the church when motivated by the excitement of people stories.

10. The congregation might have a person or several persons serve as "reporters" on what their money is accomplishing. They should view their assignment with the same sense of excitement as the people who look at the stock report first thing in the morning to see how their investments are doing. This kind of lively reporting can be infectious and raise the level of interest and excitement over investing in the church.

Don't be too quick to decide that one or several or all of the above ideas won't work. The world is filled with people who are sure that something won't work because "it's been tried before," or "it's never been done that way before."

One person called it "unreal" to think that congregations would appoint reporters on projects supported by church. He couldn't imagine that happening. It had never been done before. That same person also was quite sure that congregations would not come out for an evening of storytelling—until one wintry night when streets were treacherous with ice and snow and sleet, and 800 people paid five dollars each to attend such an event. Increasingly, congregations are finding it quite workable to encourage members to take advantage of their vacations, visiting at least one institution, agency, or project supported by the congregation, bringing the greetings of the congregation, then reporting back to the congregation. With the increase in global travel, it takes only a little extra effort for members of congregations to include a visit to one of the overseas projects supported by the congregation.

The 10 ideas listed in this chapter are just that, ideas. They are not laws guaranteed to work for everyone on every occasion. They are mind stretchers, intended to stimulate other ideas, especially in the minds of those people who are convinced that the story of the church and its expression in stewardship can be exciting.

9

TESTIMONIALS

The barber and the box

An attorney tells this story about his barber.

For years he had been going to a certain barber. Every time he paid him the attorney noticed that the barber would take some coins out the cash register and put them in a box on top of the register. The attorney never questioned the practice.

One day the conversation had been kind of jovial, and for seemingly no reason at all the attorney said to the barber, "Jim, I notice that whenever I pay, you always put some coins in the box up there. What's that for? To buy your wife some flowers or something?"

The barber seemed hesitant, but mumbled, "No, that's for the . . ." The last words were mumbled.

"What did you say?" the attorney asked.

"That's for the . . . ." And again the last word was mumbled.

The attorney looked the barber straight in the face and said, "Look, Jim, this may be none of my business, but I'm interested. Do you want to tell me what you use that money for?"

"Well," the barber drawled sheepishly, "You see, years ago I decided to tithe, so everytime someone pays me for cutting his hair, I just take 10 percent of it and put it in this box up here. It's for the Lord."

For him tithing was as simple as that. He had made a commitment.

The attorney never forgot the story. And it caused him to do a little reflecting about his own stewardship.

The professor

He was a retired professor at a church college and had never known a very large salary. But he loved his church. Once when the national church body was having a special fund appeal, he was approached about making a special gift.

"Well, let me see," he said. "We'd like to support it. But I am on a fixed income, and it's somewhat minimal. Pension and Social Security, you know. We get along. Let's see here, I keep a running account of all of our income, expenses, and contributions. My contributions to the church and similar causes total about 18 percent right now, and there's still about a half a year to go. What do you think I should cut out, so I can contribute to this special appeal?"

"We really don't want you to cut anything out," the solicitor said. "This appeal is an 'over and above,' request. I certainly understand your situation, and I don't want to put any pressure on you. Not knowing your circumstances, I just wanted to give you an opportunity to contribute if you felt so inclined."

"My wife and I really are supportive of this cause," the retired professor said. "I'll tell you what, I'll talk it over with her and let you know."

Shortly thereafter they gave their answer. "We'll give $5000," he said. "I'm not quite sure where it's going to come from, but somehow or other, we'll make it."

After several months the retired professor called again. "I've got it all figured out," he said. "We got a three percent cost of living adjustment in our social security and we've been living comfortably on what we have been getting, so we don't really need that. And then I had made a loan to a church some years ago, which I had forgotten about. This week I got notice of an interest payment that I'm going to get, and that together with the COLA from Social Security is just enough to make the $5000."

The wheat rancher

He was a wheat rancher and a committed churchman. He served on various boards of his congregation in his district and the national body. He was not a man of many words and he could not boast of a college education, but that lack in no way inhibited him from talking for the Lord whenever the opportunity came.

He never felt he had to have the latest equipment on his ranch, so he was careful not to go into too much debt and was somewhat critical of others who did.

"I can't see why you need a four-wheel-drive pickup truck to go into town on a dry road to get a cup of coffee," he used to say.

He looked for ways to put his money to good use in the church. It started in a small way.

"I heard of a new mission church being started, and it needed a couple of thousand dollars to get over the hump. I could easily supply that. It made me feel good. Later I heard of another church that needed a bit more help than I could give alone. So I talked to a couple other members of the church and our congregation decided to help sponsor another mission. And so it went. I guess that's what the Lord put us on this earth for, to be helpful to others. After all, all that I have is a gift from the Lord, so why shouldn't I use it to his glory in ways that will make it possible for other people to hear about him? When other people see me coming, they sometimes turn away, afraid that I'm going to ask them to give to the church. And maybe I overdo it sometimes. But I just like to have others experience the same joy in giving that I have."

Fred

Let's call him Fred. That's not his real name. But he is a real person, and he is a committed member of the church. He likes to support it, as well as numerous other worthwhile causes. In all, he gives about 10 percent of his income to these causes, about three-fourths of it to the church.

For a number of years now his church has been growing in stewardship and has been increasing its budget, suggesting that the members increase their percentage of giving to the church by an equal amount.

If there is anyone who could feel excused from this request, Fred certainly could. While he had a comfortable income, it had never been exorbitant, barely over $30,000 a year. Besides, his wife was in a nursing home, which cost him about $20,000 a year, $12,000 of which he had to pay out of his own pocket.

Every now and then he would get a small contract in addition to his regular work for which he was paid a consultant's fee. That seemed to come every time he was just at the point where he thought he might have to cut his pledge to the church.

It occurred to him that if God took care of him in this way, perhaps he could also increase his pledge to the church and other causes to over 10 percent. He decided to do so. Every year it went up, until finally it got to 20 percent. Now he can hardly believe that he is able to do this. He certainly doesn't require that everyone must follow his example. He simply shares what he has decided to do and the excitement he derives from doing it.

Tin can on a shelf

They were poor and their years were running out. When as their new pastor I first met them, they were living in neat makeshift quarters in the warehouse where he worked as night janitor. They had no car, but on Sunday morning, arm in arm, they trudged their way to the church.

As I sat in the chair she offered me, my eye caught sight of a tin can on a shelf, a place that normally would have been reserved for a family picture. She saw me looking at it and with a smile told me that that was where their weekly offering to the Lord was kept. Her husband made $19 a week, she said, and the first thing he did after he got his paycheck was to put $1.90 in the can. Never have I been able to forget the feeling of wonder, admiration, and pity—and shame for myself—that overcame me that day.

I asked myself, "What power is there that causes two people to pray, 'Give us this day our daily bread,' and to believe that God does answer? What inner springs are there that bring gratitude and patience and trust into lives that with good reason could retreat into bitterness, anxiety, and even despair?"

Once I thought to tell them that the church certainly could get along without their $1.90. But I never did. They had learned the Lord's lesson, which is so hard for us to learn, that it is more blessed to give than to receive. I'm sure that the $1.90 they emptied from their can each week gave more joy than the $17.10 they had left.

Retirement stewardship

They were an aging couple, not elderly, but aging as all of us are. In their early sixties, they were now ready for retirement. One might not call them wealthy, but they were certainly financially comfortable. They had always watched their money carefully, not overly frugal, but not spendthrifts either. And now that the husband was retiring, they were assured that their pensions, savings, and Social Security would see them through without any lowering of their standard of living.

Then a seminary professor, whom they greatly admired, called on them for a gift to the seminary. Of course, they would be glad to do this. They had always been liberal in their contributions to the church. But they were a little taken aback when the professor suggested a gift of $10,000. They had never thought in those terms, particularly now that they were entering retirement with a reduced income.

But they loved the seminary and the church and they wanted to help. A financial consultant showed them how by spreading their gift out over several years, it would actually provide them with a tax benefit. He also pointed out that by calling attention to the tax benefit he was not advocating that as their motivation for giving. The motivation was there already. The tax laws simply made it possible for them to do what they really wanted to do.

They reported afterwords that they simply had never thought of themselves as being capable of that kind of gift and only regretted that they had not thought in those terms earlier. It was a joyful and exciting experience for them.

The businessman

After the Sunday sermon, a businessman made an appointment with his pastor.

"Pastor," he said, "I've got a question to ask you. You preached about stewardship of talents. I've tried it, but it just doesn't seem to work for me.

"I've served on the evangelism committee, but it just never seemed to work out for me. You know that I love my church. I'm here every Sunday and I'm interested in getting other people to come. But somehow I just don't seem to be able to go to other people and talk with them about the Lord. Maybe that's my fault, but I have really tried.

"I love kids, especially high school kids. So I offered to teach a high school class in Sunday school. But I'm just no good at it.

"You know what I'm really good at? I'm good at making money. I enjoy it. I make lots of it, and I do it honestly. Is it possible that that's the best stewardship of my talents? I make lots of money and I like to give a lot of money to the church. I wish I were a good Sunday school teacher too, but I'm not. And I know the importance of good evangelism. But maybe I don't have that special gift. Is it really possible that my best gift is to make money, and that I can use that for the Lord?"

It is possible that this series of stories—the barber, the retired professor, the rancher, etc.—will do the exact opposite of what I encouraged earlier in the book. There I said that the church too often views stewardship of money in a context of guilt rather than the excitement of giving and investing. And so when I hear these stories I come away with a sense of guilt, because the example of these people put me to shame.

But they need not. Does a teenage boy, crazy about sports, feel guilty because he can't play quite as well as the year's leading home-run hitter in the major leagues? No. But he does feel a sense of excitement as he looks at what star players are doing and hopes that someday he may be like one of them. They are heroes to him and inspire him. Perhaps in the same way we all need heroes of stewardship, not to make us feel guilty, but to inspire us to excitement.

God uses all kinds of people—poor, middle class, and wealthy—and does not compare one with the other. God forgives our shame and calls us to a life of exciting stewardship that is even more powerful than guilt.